ONCE UPON A MOLECULE
by George T. Javor

7682

Southern Publishing Association, Nashville, Tennessee

This book was
Edited by Gerald Wheeler
Designed by Mark O'Connor
Cover designed by John Simpson
Cover photograph by John Halliburton,
Vanderbilt University

Type set: 10/12 Optima

Printed in U.S.A.

Library of Congress Cataloging in Publication Data

Javor, George T   1940-
    Once upon a molecule.

    Bibliography: p.
    1. Life—Origin.   2. Life (Biology)   3. Chemical
evolution.   4. Evolution and religion.   I. Title.
QH325.J38   577   78-27359
ISBN 0-8127-0227-1

Contents

On the Small Matter of Life

A policeman on his night beat encountered an obviously inebriated individual crawling around a lamppost.

"What are you doing here?" the officer inquired.

"I am looking for the quarter I dropped," came the answer from below.

"And just where did you lose your quarter?"

"About two blocks from here."

"Then tell me, my good man, why are you looking for your money here?"

"Because there is more light here."

Current attempts to explain what life is about in terms of chemistry come as close to their goal as the tipsy person in the story above. And perhaps for similar reasons. Scientists are searching for clues about life, using concepts and techniques which they are comfortable with, but which may be inadequate for such a task.

A visit to the technical journal section of a university library should quickly convince anyone that a veritable flood of scientific information pours out on a weekly and monthly basis. Periodicals burst at the covers with reports of the latest results from thousands of laboratories all over the world. A large share of them involve research on living and once-living matter. The latter half of the twentieth century is witnessing a knowledge explosion in biochemistry, the science that studies the workings of living matter on the fundamental level of molecules and atoms.

Our increased know-how in biochemistry has produced much good. We can explain formerly mysterious and crippling diseases as resulting from a lack of a specific substance and can scientifically remedy such deficiencies. Science has learned how to deal with poisons and has learned to identify and eliminate potentially harmful substances in our environments. Medicine has become more of a science and less of an art today, partly because of the contribution of biochemistry.

The knowledge explosion in biochemistry, however, also fueled the rise of a new branch of the materialistic philosophy of evolution, called chemical or biochemical evolution. Biochemical evolution operates on a simple premise. If we know the chemical makeup of living matter, then we should be able to explain how such substances came into existence originally and, moreover, duplicate the original events in a modern laboratory setting.

Behind the efforts of biochemical evolutionists lies the firm conviction that matter alone contains the inherent principles of life and that life inevitably blossoms forth if conditions in nature are favorable for such an occurrence.

For a time scientists busied themselves creating artificial life. In 1892 a man named Bütschli mixed olive oil with potash and obtained amoebalike particles. Another scientist, Leduc, compounded molten calcium chloride with a saturated solution of potassium phosphate in 1928 to produce algaelike structures. Also in the 1920s a Russian, Oparin, attempted to create cell-like structures from protein and gum arabic. However, no scientist has transformed nonliving substance into living matter. And the zest to create living matter from nonliving largely vanished as science better understood the composition and arrangement of living matter.

We now know that all forms of living matter consist of cells. Fundamental units of life, they occur in many sizes and degrees of complexity. Some organisms, such as the simple bacteria, are a single self-sufficient cell. Other more complex forms of life are a collection of millions and even billions of diverse types of specialized cells, united to work for the welfare of the whole organism.

There are as many different kinds of cells as there are organisms (estimated to be two million different species). We can see some cells, such as a hen's egg or a cell on the surface of the skin, with the unaided eye, while others, such as the bacterium, are so tiny that only powerful microscopes can bring them into view.

The many diverse forms of life, however, have a remarkably similar composition. All known matter, living or nonliving, consists of combinations of fundamental ingredients called elements. Elements cannot be changed or broken down to anything simpler in the chemical laboratory. They include such well-known substances as carbon, copper, gold, hydrogen, iron, silver, nitrogen, and oxygen.

Ancient Greek philosophers, speculating on the nature of matter, decided that it must be made up of invisible particles that cannot be cut to smaller pieces. They named the imaginary particles *atomos,* meaning "not cut." Modern science confirmed their theories with certain modifications. Today we know that an atom is the smallest possible unit of a given element. Different atoms make up different elements. There exist as many different types of atoms as of elements. Atoms are incredibly small. A half ounce of gold contains enough gold atoms to supply at least ten thousand billion of them to every man, woman, and child living on earth. In 1970 man could for the first time actually see the atoms of an element, the metal thorium, through a scanning electron microscope. They appeared as bright, fuzzy spots without too much detail. The continuous vibrational motion of the atoms caused the fuzziness.

Different atoms may join one another by what scientists term chemical bonds to form permanent groups called molecules. Most known matter does not consist of pure elements but of combinations of diverse elements combined into compounds. Compounds contain elements in fixed proportions. Just as the atom is the smallest unit of an element, molecules (combinations of atoms) form the fundamental building blocks of compounds.

The number of possible combinations of atoms and, thus, of the kinds of molecules that can exist, is limitless. Hundreds or even thousands of atoms may join to form one molecule. The remarkable thing about the chemical nature of living matter is that only seven elements make up 99 percent of our living tissue. In order of their importance they are oxygen, carbon, hydrogen, nitrogen, phosphorus, calcium, and sulfur. Six of the elements comprise only about 4 percent of the earth crust. Contrary to what one might expect, living matter does not consist of the elements most readily available on our earth.

The uniformity of composition among the diverse types of living matter does not stop on the level of the elements but carries through to the types of molecules as well. Water makes up about 70 percent of all living matter. In the absence of water all life processes cease.

Freeze-drying bacterial cells dramatically illustrate this fact. It appears that the process does not damage the microorganisms but simply places them in a state of suspended animation. A small heap of powderlike material is all that remains of millions of bacteria after the freeze-drying, and the cells can remain in that state for an indefinite period. When water fortified with suitable nutrients is added, microorganisms resume their normal growth. Multicellular organisms or more complex cells, however, cannot survive freeze-drying because it scrambles the internal organization beyond the possibility of repair. (Because living tissue has such a large percentage of water, we can truly observe that "we are all wet"!)

The 30 percent or so of a cell remaining after the removal of water is mostly large molecules. By large, we mean complexes formed by thousands of atoms. There are four classes of such "macromolecules": the proteins, the nucleic acids, the polysaccharides, and the lipids. Chemical analysis of living matter also reveals the presence of a few percent minerals and of smaller molecules composed of fifty or less atoms.

The macromolecules, especially the proteins and nucleic acids, "operate" the living cell. Scientists have carefully determined their chemical compositions. (A detailed description of them falls outside the scope of our discussion.) But here we encounter a paradox. The scientific world still cannot define what we mean by "living." We can tell what the composition of living matter is, can describe life, but we cannot define it.

One would think that most everybody could decide

whether an organism is alive or dead. Naturally, one looks for telltale signs of life, such as movement; response to stimuli, warmth, noise; incorporation of food; and replication or reproduction. But, alas, some inanimate objects can perform one or several of the above-mentioned tasks.

Paul Weiss, a well-known American biologist, wrote a tongue-in-cheek story entitled "Life on Earth (by a Martian)." It seems that some Martians came to visit the earth in search of life. After lengthy and careful observation of our planet, they concluded that life did indeed exist here, and furthermore, one form was dominant. They named it the "Earthian" and faithfully chronicled its every particular. Apparently the Earthians had intricate, symmetrical bodies, they moved, emitted heat and sounds, and ate (mostly liquid food). Sometimes they divided, and they eventually died. Which organism did the Martians observe? Why, automobiles, of course. In addition they also noticed associated with the Earthians some rather unimpressive structures. The Martians concluded that the latter were some kind of parasites, unworthy of further study.

Our ability to determine whether an object is alive or not rests on our previous experience with it. If we landed on a strange planet and faced the task of deciding whether life is present, we, too, would find it difficult, to say the least. Recently the United States sent two automated laboratories to the surface of Mars to determine if living organisms existed there. The results of the biology experiments strongly suggested some kind of biological activity on Mars. In an earth-based laboratory, the results would have constituted unequivocal proof for the presence of life. Yet scientists, interpreting the data radioed back from Mars, had to admit that probably Mars had no life. Chemical analyses of the Martian surface indicated the total lack of carbon-containing molecules other than carbon dioxide gas. It seems that nonliving matter on the Martian surface can mimic some of the chemical changes that here on earth are unique to living systems. In other words, even the carefully designed biological experiments intended to demonstrate the presence or absence of life on the red planet were not equal to such a task.

Another story tells about an imaginary civilization that developed a high degree of know-how in the area of chemical analysis. They could take just about any substance and rapidly determine its exact chemical composition down to the last molecule. But strangely enough, this civilization never created any system of reading or writing. When their archaeologists unearthed a book, they rapidly set about to determine its chemical nature. And that was the limit of what they could learn from the book.

It may be that when it comes to an understanding of life, we, too, cannot "read" living matter. Our biochemical approach perhaps misses an entire dimension essential to understanding the problem of life.

In summary we note that scientists are not only unable to produce living matter in the laboratory, but they cannot even define accurately what life is. In the absence of such definition, they cannot test for life in a way that will produce clear-cut results. Yet the majority of those same scientists accept the "biochemical evolution" that purports to give a step-by-step account of how life originated on our planet.

11

Old Chemists Never Die

Old chemists never die, they just come to equilibrium. Equilibrium is a state of affairs in which the status quo does not change and some sort of balance exists among the components of a system. In chemistry it refers to chemical reactions that have already run their courses. The sum total of the thousands of chemical alterations that go on in a live cell at any given moment, however, never adds up to equilibrium.

It is only away from equilibrium that chemical reactions can be controlled, accelerated, or slowed down according to the needs of the living matter. Moreover, chemical reactions that yield energy have the potential to do so only when they are not in equilibrium. When total chemical equilibrium does set in, the living thing dies.

In view of the importance for living matter not to be at a chemical equilibrium, it is paradoxical that all chemical changes in life processes happen in the presence of biological catalysts, called enzymes, that vigorously push individual reactions toward equilibrium.

A chemical change occurs when atoms grouped into one type of molecule rearrange to form different molecules. It involves breaking of old chemical bonds and forming new ones. If the new chemical bonds take less energy to maintain than the old ones, the excess energy not needed by the new molecules becomes available to the living matter to fuel its different activities.

It appears that most chemical events necessary for life require energy. The building of the macromolecules that make up the largest part of the living matter, the gathering in of the nutrients from the environment, mechanical motion, and the maintenance of a nonequilibrium state within the cell all require such chemical reactions. In fact, the living cell needs energy simply to stay intact. In the absence of a continuous supply, the typical cell rapidly disintegrates into its components.

That is why we, along with all other life forms, need food to exist. Food contains three categories of energy-rich molecules: carbohydrates, lipids, and proteins. Each cell breaks the energy-rich substances down to molecules of low energy content, carbon dioxide, and water.

The energy found in carbohydrates, proteins, and lipids came originally from the sun. Light energy reaches us from a distance of more than ninety million miles away in space. Chlorophyll and other plant pigments trap and package it into stable, chemical energy-bearing food molecules. Of course, nonplant food sources do exist, but their energy also originated in plants. Most of the two million or so species of life on earth run on solar energy!

The activity of the molecules within the cells reminds one of a high-wire act, in which only constant attention and vigilance on the part of the performer keeps him from tumbling. Likewise, living matter constantly needs a supply of energy to prevent the sum total of chemical reactions from attaining equilibrium.

How does energy keep living matter from reaching chemical equilibrium? The thousands of chemical reactions occurring moment by moment do not happen in

13

isolation from each other. On the contrary, the end product of one reaction becomes the starting material for the next. We may illustrate a hypothetical series of chemical reactions as follows: molecule A changes to molecule B, the reaction abbreviated as $A \rightarrow B$. Then $B \rightarrow C$, $C \rightarrow D$ and $D \rightarrow E$. Four chemical reactions have transformed molecule A into molecule E. It could happen that the first reaction, $A \rightarrow B$, has no chance to go to equilibrium because as soon as B appears the cell further modifies it to C. If molecule C has a higher energy content than B, the conversion of B to C would happen only if energy entered the system. In the absence of energy the reaction $A \rightarrow B$ would come to a grinding halt as equilibrium would set in.

To put it another way, certain key reactions require energy. Without it they cannot facilitate the smooth, steady flow of molecules through the various channels of metabolic pathways.

Living things organize matter into increasingly complex hierarchies. The simplest molecules are the so-called precursors of biomolecules: carbon dioxide, ammonia, water, and nitrogen. They are all freely available in the atmosphere and soil. The cells use them to manufacture slightly more complex intermediates, which in turn serve as the components for the "building block" molecules. The most important biomolecules—proteins, nucleic acids, lipids, and polysaccharides—the cell will put together from the building block molecules of amino acids, nucleotides, fatty acids, plus glycerol and simple sugars.

The cell then takes the large biomolecules and combines them into even greater supramolecular complexes and eventually organelles. It is on the level of organelles that the components of the living matter become routinely visible under the electron microscope. Even then it must magnify them many thousands of times. One of the organelles is the extensive membrane system that subdivides the interior of the cell into numerous compartments and separates a cell from its surroundings.

A vitally important fact about compartments is that their contents differ from that of their neighbors. One side of the membrane, for example, may be exposed to a high salt concentration; the other side to a lower one. Consequently, a "concentration gradient" would exist across the membrane. Such a state runs contrary to the spontaneous tendency of salt and other substances to equalize their concentrations on both sides of the membrane. Maintaining a concentration gradient across a membrane requires energy and a one-directional pumping mechanism that can transport substances through the membrane and collect them on one side.

Building large biomolecules, supramolecular complexes, and organelles requires a considerable part of the cell's material resources. One would imagine that once the cell constructed them, it would use them as long as possible. Scientists, in fact, guessed that it was the case until the 1940s and later, when isotopes (specially tagged atoms) entered biochemical research. They enabled the scientist to keep track of individual molecules. Scientists soon learned that the cell periodically breaks down all the complex molecules to the building block level and replaces them with new macromolecules. The phenomenon, called metabolic turnover, greatly minimizes the chances of partially worn-out, malfunctioning components operating in the cell. It reminds one of the prosperous car owner who trades in his vehicle every year for a new one in order to ensure totally trouble-free driving.

By mechanically rupturing the cell membranes we can collect a cell's contents one by one. The cell ceases to exist, and its components, while still able to carry on isolated chemical conversions, are in reality now a lifeless collection of molecules. If we bring all the cell parts together in a test tube and give them time, will they organize themselves into a coordinated, functioning cell? Laboratory experience shows that nothing of the sort happens. One may wait a day, a year, or even ten years, but it will never happen. Instead, the complex organelles of the cell will one by one disintegrate into successively simpler molecules. In other words, individual cell components do not strive to be part of a living system. To the inert molecules it does not seem to matter whether they participate in chemical reactions of living or nonliving matter. Current biochemical approaches to evolution, however, have the tacit understanding that individual biomolecules, once formed, will tend to merge together into a living system.

A live cell, then, is more than merely the sum of its parts. We quite frankly do not know what the extra quality is that makes a cell "live" after all its parts have joined together. Some scientists maintain that it is all a matter of correct organization of the components. By components, they usually mean the large macromolecular complexes. Therefore, according to this view, if one could assemble all the cell parts bit by bit into their proper positions until we have a three dimensional replica of the original live cell, then cell-copy would be living by virtue of its internal structure. Because we do not have the technical

16

know-how to manipulate single molecules, we cannot verify the hypothesis by experiment. And, as mentioned above, molecular complexes do not automatically self-organize into a live cell.

But were it possible for us to arrange the large molecular complexes correctly into a three-dimensional replica of a cell, our effort would most likely yield us only a dead cell. In order for us to have a live cell, a state of nonequilibrium would have to exist among the thousands of small molecules that are also part of the system. When we bring large and small molecules together in a test tube, many of the large molecules (enzymes) rapidly create equilibrium among the small molecules. Therefore an undesirable equilibrium would set in during the actual process of building the cell replica.

If this is correct, then in order to create a live cell, not only would we have to position all of the large molecular complexes in a correct three-dimensional array, but we would also need to restrain the small molecules in a state of nonequilibrium. Such a feat is outside the realm of even serious speculation.

The closest anyone came to suggesting how we might accomplish something like this, starting with an equilibrium system, was the famous nineteenth century British physicist, James Clerk Maxwell. He proposed that a little "demon" would stand at the gate connecting two compartments, both filled with gas molecules of equal temperature and pressure. The microscopic creature would let all slow-moving molecules into one compartment and collect all fast-moving ones in the other. Such a process would result in a temperature difference between the compartments, producing a nonequilibrium state from a

17

state of equilibrium.

Such considerations increase our appreciation for the complexities of living matter. Too frequently the popular media freely attach the term "living" or "life" to biomolecules, creating an impression among the readers that "life was created" or that scientists are on the verge of the creation of life. Nothing can be further from the truth. As continuing research reveals an ever-increasing network of the intricacies of life, man's chances of ever producing a living organism from nonliving matter in the laboratory rapidly approach nil. If the tens of thousands of modern-day scientists, with their armada of sophisticated equipment, cannot create life in the test tube, what is the likelihood that life arose spontaneously on the surface of a chaotic, "primordial" earth in the dim past?

Once Upon a Time There Was a Molecule . . .

Biochemical evolution is something of an afterthought to the modern version of biological evolution. In the nineteenth century Lamarck, Darwin, and Wallace proposed that organisms change dramatically during the course of history from simple to more complex types. Competition for survival is the chief selecting force in nature, permitting the more fit to survive and transmit its acquired characteristics to its offspring.

Several billion years ago, according to such theory, only simple, primitive organisms existed, and only with the passage of time did more and more complex forms of life appear. Close relatives of man came along in the past few million years of earth's long history.

Eventually people began pondering the origin of the earliest "primitive" forms of life. How did they come into existence, and what were their ancestors like? Oparin and Haldane logically proposed during the 1920s that the first primitive forms of life originated from nonliving matter. In the twenties science considered the makeup of cells to be rather simple, even within the realm of laboratory synthesis.

Thinking men had wondered about the origin of life for a long time. The Greek Anaxagoras (500?-428 BC) suggested that seeds of life fell to the earth with the rain. Aristotle (384-322 BC) taught that fleas, mosquitoes, mice, and similar creatures originated directly from putrefying matter, moist soil, and filth. In the Middle Ages scholars accepted Aristotle's teachings as the last word on any subject, and theologians found ways to harmonize the Scriptures with such views as well. After all, does not Genesis 1:24 read, ''God said, Let the earth bring forth the living creature: . . . and it was so''?

Only in 1860 did Louis Pasteur, using clever and convincing experiments, effectively demolish the theory of spontaneous generation of life. Current proponents of biochemical evolution agree with Pasteur's finding that life does not evolve spontaneously in our day, but they maintain that in the long-ago past the conditions on our planet were favorable for it.

Current evolutionary thinking postulates that our earth formed by condensation out of a huge dust cloud about four and a half billion years ago. The primitive earth supposedly lost its original atmosphere (assumed because we have much smaller percentages of certain gases in our atmosphere than found in the rest of the universe) and acquired a ''primordial atmosphere'' (a mixture of water vapors, ammonia, methane, and possibly other gases), belched out by the numerous active volcanoes. A warm, slightly alkaline ocean covered one tenth of the earth surface. The primordial earth's surface temperature was about 80° C. In addition, a generous stream of energy from the sun, especially in the form of strong ultraviolet radiation, bathed the planet. Electric discharges crisscrossed the atmosphere, and abundant radioactive elements released their energy everywhere.

Evolutionary scientists have followed two separate lines of thought on the appearance of life. One faction postulated a series of rapid, though improbable, events that gave rise to life more or less by chance. The concept proved unsatisfying to many because it did not permit scientific experimentation. The other approach—the one currently enjoying popularity—assumes that life came about as a result of numerous, relatively slow, but probable and reproducible events, and that the emergence of life on our planet was inevitable. Such thinking does lead to laboratory experiments, allowing us to actually attempt to verify it by scientific methods.

A Nobel prize laureate, H. Urey, and one of his graduate students, S. Miller, took the first serious experimental approach to biochemical evolution at the University of Chicago in the early 1950s. They sealed two electrodes into a large glass flask. The flask, connected to a distilling apparatus and equipped with a cold trap, formed a closed unit. The two men filled the flask with methane, ammonia, and hydrogen gases while water boiled continuously in the attached distilling apparatus.

With their experiment they sought to test the hypothesis that the atmosphere of the earth was the most likely place where the first biologically important molecules appeared. The gases introduced into the reaction chamber were those thought to surround the primordial earth. For about a week they passed electrical discharges through the gas mixture, simulating primordial lightning. Any chemical substance produced became trapped in the liquid portion of the distillation apparatus. By the end of the experiment the solution had turned to a red color, indicating the presence of organic matter. When Urey and Miller analyzed its contents, they found a number of interesting biological substances, including four types of amino acids: glycine, alanine, aspartic acid, and glutamic acid. Since the all-important macromolecules, proteins, consist of amino acids, the results of the experiment represented a signal triumph for biochemical evolution.

Soon other laboratories produced amino acids in simulated primordial atmospheres as well. Different scientists used various mixtures of gases and a variety of energy sources. Besides ammonia, methane, hydrogen, and water they tried nitrogen, hydrogen cyanide, carbon dioxide, acetic acid, hydrogen, hydrogen sulfide, ethylene, and formaldehyde. As for sources of energy, they utilized ultraviolet radiation, heat, shock waves, gamma radiation, and electron beams. Different starting conditions yielded different amino acids. Out of the twenty different types of amino acids found in proteins today, science has produced eighteen in simulated primordial-type atmospheres.

Moreover, not only have they synthesized the precursor molecules of proteins, but of lipids, polysaccharides, and nucleic acids. It required different starting materials and experimental conditions to produce them, though. Thus it appears that a substantial body of experimental evidence has accumulated to bolster the biochemical evolutionary hypothesis.

A closer examination of what science has actually accomplished, however, leaves one less than convinced about what the experiments imply. First, the design of the apparatus tilts the results in favor of what the scientists hope to achieve and does not faithfully reflect the postulated primordial conditions. If gas molecules of the primordial atmosphere interacted to form precursor molecules under the influence of an energy source, these same molecules could just as well disintegrate while still under the same conditions. In the laboratory experiment, the scientists removed the amino acids or other precursor-type molecules as soon as they were formed. Thus the experimental environment had no chance to break the molecules down as the actual situation would.

A yet more serious objection to the relevance of the experiments to primordial conditions is that the scientists have deliberately excluded the gas oxygen from the reaction chamber. Our atmosphere currently contains 21 percent oxygen, and without it, a large fraction of all living beings would cease to exist. Nevertheless, oxygen is a potentially troublesome substance for the biochemical evolutionist. The presence of oxygen will allow only formic acid, acetic acid, and other highly oxidized molecules to form. They are useless to the evolutionist.

Many of the important molecules of life are in a highly "reduced" state, meaning they contain relatively few oxygen atoms for each carbon atom in a given molecule. Such substances have a tendency to react with oxygen relatively rapidly, converting to biologically worthless matter.

All living matter existing in a highly oxygenated atmosphere, such as ours, needs to contain elaborate enzyme systems to protect against the harmful effects of oxygen. Microorganisms without the defense mechanisms are "obligate anaerobes." Simple exposure to air kills them. Evolutionists postulate that anaerobes most resemble the first living organisms on earth. As evolution progressed, photosynthetic organisms supposedly appeared on the scene. The plants released oxygen into the atmosphere as an end product of their metabolism.

23

Photosynthesis is a complex process that converts water and carbon dioxide gas into oxygen and sugarlike compounds called carbohydrates. The plant harnesses the energy needed for such biochemical work from light. The process of photosynthesis traps a portion of the sun's radiant energy in the carbohydrates. Burning carbohydrates (such as the log in the fireplace) or metabolizing them as food releases the energy. At the same time the chemical reaction consumes oxygen—using exactly as much during the burning of a given quantity of carbohydrate as its photosynthesis produced earlier. Most plant material eventually ends up decomposing one way or another back to carbon dioxide and water, resulting in no net oxygen production. The release of oxygen during photosynthesis and its use during burning and decomposition balance each other.

The only plausible way that the earth can gain atmospheric oxygen from photosynthetic activities in the long run is to bury the plant material before it has a chance to decay. Such burials did occur, as the extensive oil and coal deposits testify, but many of the burials likely occurred rather rapidly instead of being the gradual affairs that geology has traditionally taught. As a result, it is difficult to imagine a slow increase in atmospheric oxygen. If, on the other hand, the oxygenless atmosphere rapidly changed into an oxygenated one, it would have killed all organisms present on earth unless they had the necessary mechanisms to cope with oxygen.

Current evidence suggests that the theory of a primordial earth enveloped in an oxygenless atmosphere at any time during its history will simply not hold up. We now know that the high-energy ultraviolet radiation of the sun can shatter the water molecules present in the upper atmosphere, releasing hydrogen and oxygen gases in a process called the photodissociation of water. Calculations made by R. T. Brinkman of the California Institute of Technology indicate that the earth should have had oxygen present in its atmosphere for more than 99 percent of our planet's postulated evolutionary history.

G. R. Carruthers obtained direct evidence for the importance of the photodissociation of water through the scientific experiments of the Apollo 16 mission in 1972. A special camera placed on the surface of the moon captured some two hundred frames of our earth and its atmosphere as it appears in the far ultraviolet region of the spectrum. The pictures revealed that a large cloud of hydrogen extending 40,000 miles into space surrounds the earth. Such an enormous quantity of hydrogen must have originated from the ongoing process of photodissociation of water. (Radioactive carbon production in the atmosphere also yields some hydrogen, but on a much smaller scale.) Hydrogen gas, being the lightest substance in existence, escapes our atmosphere, whereas the heavier oxygen remains behind. The news release of the discovery from the Naval Research Laboratory in Washington, D.C., stated in part: "Solar effects on the earth's water that evaporates to the high atmosphere may provide our primary supply of oxygen and not photosynthesis as is generally believed."

Recent data from the atmosphere of Venus indicates the presence of measurable quantities of atomic oxygen there as well. Scientists think it came from the photodissociation of carbon dioxide.

Clearly, the production of oxygen on a primordial-type earth invalidates all presently postulated schemes of biochemical evolution, including those that begin with the Miller-Urey type of atmospheric synthesis of biological precursor molecules.

A number of evolutionary scientists recognize the difficulty of their position. They are turning increasingly to alternative suggestions, such as the one made by Dr. G. Arrhenius of the University of California, San Diego. He proposes that organic matter or even some life forms could have existed in the solar system before the earth did. During the formation of our planet the particles coalescing to form the earth could have captured some of the organic matter. In other words, the components of life or life itself could have been "imported" from outer space.

Lest we think that the idea is a radically new "solution" to the age-old question of the origin of life, we must remember that the Greek Anaxagoras proposed in the fifth century BC that "seeds of life fell to the earth with the rain." Science has not progressed far toward solving this problem in the ensuing twenty-five hundred years.

The Sum of the Matter

The creation-evolution controversy is more than a purely academic squabble. Whether realized or not, it has ideological implications. The side one chooses in the debate can well shape his entire outlook on existence. It does make a difference whether life exists on earth as an outworking of the will and purpose of the Benevolent Creator or as the result of the random, mindless movements of atoms and molecules. The former notion brings one into harmony with nature through the Common Author, while the latter leads a person to look on his environment as a selective force and a potential hazard. The creationist sees order and meaning in all phases of existence—past, present, and future. To the evolutionists the past was a murky chaos, and the present is a continuous struggle for survival as well as an unrelenting march toward an unknown destiny.

Throughout history, mankind has always divided on the question of allegiance. In every age the overwhelming majority opted for paying homage to the powers of nature as the creator and sustainer. Most cultures of the past personified the phenomena into various gods, from Athena to Zeus. More recently, science has identified the forces as the fundamental laws of physics and chemistry, and evolutionists pay the same homage to them as the ancients accorded their gods. A small minority, on the other hand, have consistently maintained that a single supernatural being created the earth and the life on it.

From the standpoint of human reason, the majority view was always the more logical one. Before we understood the operation of nature in terms of physical laws, it seemed logical to postulate that powerful intelligent beings were directly running our world. For example, it made sense that a supernatural being pushed the sun across the sky every day. Such a task was obviously a full-time job, even for a god. Likewise, the numerous other manifestations of nature, the movements of clouds, the winds, the flow of rivers, the motions of stars, the growth of vegetation, the ebb and tide of oceans, the eruption of volcanoes, the earthquakes, all demanded the existence of a god in charge of each one. In contrast, it was clearly absurd to believe that a single god could cope single-handedly with everything at the same time. Again, in our day of great technical sophistication, it is much more in the spirit of our times to think that matter organized itself automatically into a variety of forms (including life) through a series of well-understood spontaneous steps than to invoke the existence of an unseen, but all-powerful creator.

Unfortunately for the evolutionist, life is not appearing from nonliving matter anywhere in the world. Therefore we cannot study the process of creation of life in a laboratory setting and by the scientific method. Someone has said that "belief is good religion but poor science." We have shown in the preceding chapters that biochemical evolution of life falls entirely into the category of "belief." Further, we noted that the acceptance of biochemical evolution demands an extraordinary capacity to believe. For we have seen that we do not understand the phenomenon called life well enough even to accurately define it, let alone to describe step by step how it came into existence. After examining the dynamics of living matter, we concluded that spontaneous processes could not create the nonequilibrium states essential for the maintenance of life. Finally, we realized that even the initial steps of biochemical evolution, the process of simple building-block molecule synthesis in a primordial atmosphere, was an impossibility because of the constant presence of oxygen.

The theory of biological evolution, the process of continuing emergence of new species of living organisms throughout the "millions of years" of earth's history, is a logical continuation of biochemical evolution. The questionable status of the latter reflects unfavorably on the former.

Creationists, on the other hand, need to understand clearly the reasons behind their adherence to the concept of special creation. They are primarily religious in nature, based on belief rather than demonstrated facts. The inability of the evolutionist to demonstrate the spontaneous emergence of life does not necessarily strengthen the case for creationism. The shaky ground under the evolutionist does not firm up the foundations of creationism. They are independent of each other. Moreover, were evolutionists able to create life in their laboratories at will, they still could not demolish the creationists' position, because the latter ideology rests on a revealed historical event that took place in the absence of human observers. At best, evolutionists could demonstrate a possible way in which we came into being.

29

The same Bible that reveals our true origins also contains the message from the Creator, "Come now, and let us reason together." Far from requiring blind, unreasoning dogmatism, God desires that the children of men perceive the impossibility of life's coming into existence spontaneously. To help us understand this and other concepts vital for the "reasoning together" process, God set in motion forces that gave rise to modern science.

Modern science revealed the physical realities to mankind. Now humanity can see the complexity behind our existence, and the painful reality of our finiteness is finally dawning upon us. There are worlds out in space that we cannot hope to reach because of the distances involved. Other worlds within the cell, within the molecules and atoms, also defy direct manipulation. At the same time our efforts to account for such phenomena solely by evolutionary reasoning have failed. Recognition of such facts is part of the reasoning process to which God invited us. In light of the above, is it totally unreasonable to accept God's own revelation of our origins?

In our finiteness we cannot comprehend, measure, analyze, and embrace the totality of God. We can merely accept His revelations to us. After learning how natural processes work, we can accept the fact that some phenomena require the existence of a designer and a creator. Therefore, logic demands the existence of just such a God as the Bible describes. "O Lord our Lord, how excellent is thy name in all the earth! who hast set thy glory above the heavens. . . . When I consider thy heavens, the work of thy fingers, the moon and the stars, which thou hast ordained; what is man, that thou art mindful of him?"

30

Bibliography

England, D. *A Christian View of Origins*. Baker Book House, 1972.

Evard, R., and D. Schrodetzki. "Chemical Evolution." *Origins,* Vol. 3 (1976), pp. 9-37.

Lehninger, A. L. *Bioenergetics*. W. A. Benjamin, Inc., 1965.

————. "The Origin of Life." *Biochemistry,* 2nd ed. Worth Publishers, Inc., 1975, pp. 1031-1056.

Marquand, J. *Life: Its Nature, Origins and Distribution*. W. W. Norton Co., Inc., 1971.

Miller, S. L., and L. E. Orgel. *The Origins of Life on the Earth*. Prentice-Hall, Inc., 1973.

Snow, G. E., and G. T. Javor. "Oxygen and Evolution." *Origins,* Vol. 2 (1975), pp. 59-63.